Glow in the Dark ROCK PAINTING

Katie Cameron

hinkler

Contents

The Wonderful Art of Painting Rocks 3

Getting Started 4

Balance Cats 8

Triangle Twinkle 10

Dream Galaxy 12

Luminosi Tree 14

Isometric Glow 16

Glow Up 18

Fantastic Fungi 20

Mermaid Moment 22

Congratulations! 24

About the Author 24

hinkler

Published by Hinkler Books Pty Ltd
45–55 Fairchild Street
Heatherton Victoria 3202 Australia
www.hinkler.com

Author: Katie Cameron
Internal design: Lisa Howard
Cover design: Sam Grimmer

ISBN: 978 1 4889 2009 7

Printed and bound in China

The Wonderful Art of Painting Rocks

Rock painting has proven itself to be a timeless craft. Long before humans could read or write, they were painting art on stone. Since these early times, painting art on rocks has taken various forms and has once more become a popular activity for people of all ages and skill levels.

Painting rocks is a great activity whatever the weather. Sunny days are great for seeking out your rock "canvases," while the task of decorating them makes for a great rainy-day activity. The possibilities for what you can paint on rocks and stones are endless. Common stones can be turned into stunning and unique works of art to be treasured, or even given as gifts to friends and family. Painted rocks can serve a range of uses such as paperweights, doorstops, or garden decor, or you can simply display your masterpieces where they can be seen and appreciated.

Many people find the act of painting stones to be calming and therapeutic and have integrated it into their meditation grounding practice. Others have taken up rock painting as a family or community activity intended to promote kindness and sharing as well as finding new ways to explore nature.

Whether this is your first experience in painting stones or you are looking for new techniques, the tutorials in this book are meant to inspire and help you learn and grow your artistic abilities. Don't be afraid to use different colors or designs to those which are described in the projects. Practice and experimentation are the best ways to develop your skills and your own unique style. You are limited only by your creativity and imagination!

HANDY HINT

Using glow-in-the-dark paint adds a whole new dimension to your rock art. You can choose to completely cover your rocks in glow paint, or just pick out special highlights—either way will add extra elements of pop and pizzazz when the lights go out!

IMPORTANT: *While there are many uses for glow paint, you should not use it on your skin or on anything that may be eaten/ingested.*

Getting Started

Here are the basic things to know when you're just starting out in the wonderful world of rock painting.

Stones

The best stones to paint on are smooth and relatively free of cracks or holes. Stones that are too rough or pitted are not ideal, as they make it difficult to paint smoothly and add fine details.

Collecting your rock "canvases" is arguably one of the most exciting parts of the rock-art process! Smooth stones are most often found along the shores of oceans and rivers; be inspired by the different shapes and sizes of the stones you find, and choose your art to suit them. If gathering your own stones isn't an option, however, or you want to save time, you can also purchase them at craft stores.

IMPORTANT: *If you're collecting stones yourself, make sure it's okay to take stones from that area. Some public places have regulations that prevent you taking things away, to protect the environment or to be respectful of a local culture, or both! If you're taking stones from private property, ensure that you always ask permission from the owner.*

Thoroughly clean your stones before you start painting them. Rinse off any mud or sand outside (not down the kitchen drain!), then give them a scrub in the sink with soap and water, and leave them to dry completely before you begin.

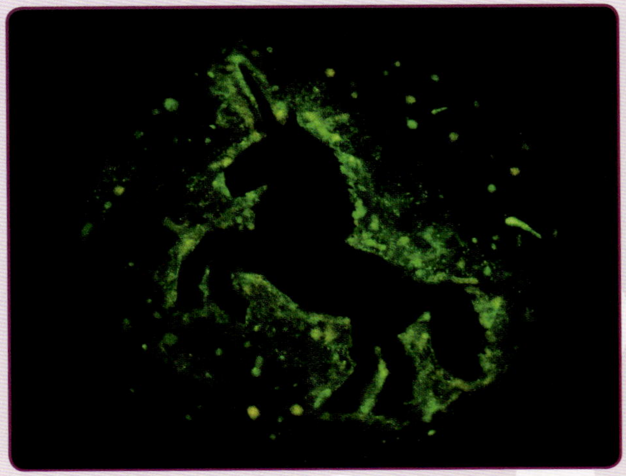

Glow-in-the-Dark Paint

Glow-in-the-dark paint is also known as "phosphorescent paint," "luminous paint," or simply "glow paint." It's a type of paint that you can see in the dark (obviously!), and is created using man-made luminescent phosphors such as zinc oxide or strontium aluminate. When you shine light on these chemicals, they absorb and store the light energy and then release it gradually.

Don't confuse glow paint with neon paint or fluorescent paint. Though these paints look very bright during daylight and will "glow" under a UV blacklight, once all lights are out you won't be able to see them. Glow paint will glow under a UV light and will also visibly glow with no lights on at all.

Glow paint won't glow forever without some recharging, of course! Just expose the paint to light (from a bright light bulb, a UV blacklight, or sunshine) to recharge it. The good news is that you can do this over and over—there's no limit to the amount of times you can recharge the paint. Your creations will always be ready to glow again, after they've been exposed to light!

Here are some helpful tips for using glow paint:

- Try out your glow paint before starting, as not all glow paint is the same. You'll want to test for things like thickness and opacity, so you can determine how much paint to put on your brush and how many layers you need to get a good glow on.
- Glow paint tends to work best—that is, you need fewer coats and it looks brighter for longer—when it's applied over white or light-colored backgrounds.
- Avoid uneven glow (caused by streaks or raised edges) by using less glow paint on your brush and applying thin coats, adding more as needed. Also, give your glow paint a little extra time to dry between coats: 10 to 15 minutes or more, depending on the thickness of the coat.
- Don't mix glow paint with regular paint—this will reduce the glow effect when the lights are out. Regular acrylic paint is opaque and will block the light from charging the glow particles.

HANDY HINT

Check your glow-paint work as you go. If you have a UV blacklight, you can see the paint's glow as you apply it, in a room with dim lighting. If you don't have a blacklight, check on how your art is progressing by charging the paint for 10 to 20 seconds under a bright light, then turning out the lights in a dark room.

Generally, unless you have glow paint pre-tinted in a particular color, it will dry clear or a bit cloudy; but with the lights out, it typically glows a yellow-green color. This is due to the use of zinc sulfide, the chemical that gives the paint its glowing abilities. If you want your art to glow in colors other than yellow-green, your best bet is to try adding layers of glow paint over bright and neon colors. Using a UV blacklight will also brighten any colors you use, though technically they won't glow in the dark.

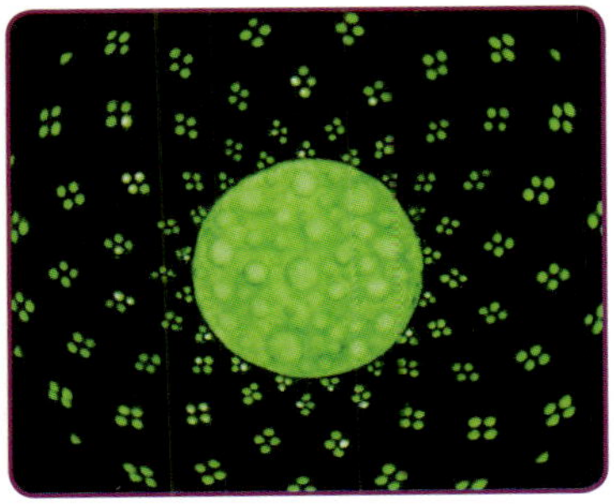

Acrylic Paint

Regular "craft" or "student" acrylic paint works very well for painting the non-glowing part of your artwork. It's non-toxic, fast-drying, and adheres well to a stone's surface; it's also cheap to purchase and easy to clean up using a little soap and water.

Most acrylic paint is easily intermixable, too. You can mix new color combinations or add a little bit of black paint to darken a color, or a little white paint to lighten up.

Tools

There are a few other tools that are useful to have when creating glow-in-the-dark rocks.

Paintbrushes

You'll also need paintbrushes. The most useful brushes for rock painting are synthetic, pointed, round brushes, which are best for fine detailing and lines, dotting, and touch-ups. Use a larger round or flat brush to paint areas that need more coverage, like base coats and backgrounds.

Take care of your paintbrushes so that they keep their shape and do not fray. Try not to dip them into paint further than half the bristle length, and never allow them to dry with paint still on them. Keep a little cup of water at your work station so that you can quickly swish off the paint and keep the bristles moist, before washing them with soap and water.

Pencil and Eraser

Use these to sketch out your ideas and designs on paper beforehand. Light markings in a gray pencil can be used directly on the stone or dry paint, and an eraser can be used to remove any marks—or you can simply paint over them.

Drawing Compass and Ruler

You can use your eye to judge measurements like center points for designs and base coats, but a ruler and compass make this process much faster and easier. Where symmetry is an important factor in creating your design, you will want precise and equal measurements on all sides. These tools will also help to guide your creative process when forming new designs on paper. A compass may be difficult to use on some shapes of stones; if this is the case, just use your judgment to visually choose the center spot.

You can also use gel pens, permanent markers, and other items like sparkles, sequins, beads, and other tiny treasures to decorate your rock art.

Tips and Tricks

Be Patient

Painted stones can take many hours, if not days, to complete, as you need to take your time when painting small design details, and it's also important to allow the paint to dry between the steps. Patience is key. Use a comfortable chair and don't rush the process.

The time it takes for the paint to dry varies. Factors like how heavily it's applied, the temperature, humidity, type of paint, and even the color used can influence drying time. Generally, you're going to be waiting five to fifteen minutes for acrylic and glow paint to be dry to touch. You can speed up drying time using a blow-dryer on low setting.

Another time-saver is to be prepared! Have your work space equipped with everything you need within arm's reach, and plan ahead by sketching out your design idea before you start. You can even trace the shape of your stone onto a piece of paper, so you can get an idea of what will fit on your "canvas."

HANDY HINT

Be aware of the time you're spending painting, and try not to sit for too long! Get up, stretch, and move around for 10 minutes or so at least once an hour. Movement is good for your body's circulation and can also help you refocus on the rock at hand.

Work Space

You need a well-lit work space and a sturdy surface (a table or desk) to paint on. Use a drop cloth or old newspaper to protect your tabletop and the surrounding area.

When you're using glow-in-the-dark paint, it's helpful to have a bright desk lamp nearby to charge the glow paint. Having the on/off switch close by makes checking your work that much quicker in a dimly lit room.

Painting Dots

Some of the designs in this kit involve painting dots. While this might sound simple enough, painting dots can be tricky without some practice. The easiest way to start out is to use a variety of dotting tools with different-sized tips to get the size of dot you want. These don't need to be store-bought tools—you can repurpose common household items like toothpicks, pencils, or chopsticks.

I find the easiest way to ensure accuracy when placing dots is to hold the stick in one hand as you would a pencil and, if needed, steady the rock with your other hand. Try to hold the stick vertically to the stone, coming in at a 90-degree angle when applying dots. Steady your aim by resting your hand, wrist, or elbow against the desk or the stone itself.

To increase the size of each dot from one row to the next is mostly a matter of having the right amount of paint on the right-sized stick. Usually, the smaller the point, the smaller the dot will be. I use the small pointed end of a toothpick. Another way to achieve very small dots is to use the very tip of the longest bristle in a round paintbrush.

The smallest dots do not require a lot of paint to be on the point to make a well-formed circle-shaped dot. Too much paint and you could accidentally place a dot too large. Generally, if you do not re-dip and use the same amount of pressure with each dot, the size of the next dot will be smaller than the one before it, so you will need to wipe clean and re-dip the stick into the paint after each dot to maintain saturation and equal dot sizing.

When you want to go up in the size of a dot, you can use the same size dotting tool saturated in slightly more paint and add just a bit more pressure while touching the stick to stone. If you do not wipe the paint from the stick before re-dipping, it will start to dry and accumulate, enlarging the end of the tool. A bigger tool end will give a bigger size dot.

To increase dot size, you can also use a larger tool. The diameter of the end of the tool you are using is a good indication of the size of the dot it will create, and of course the more it is saturated with paint, the bigger the dot will be.

Blocking

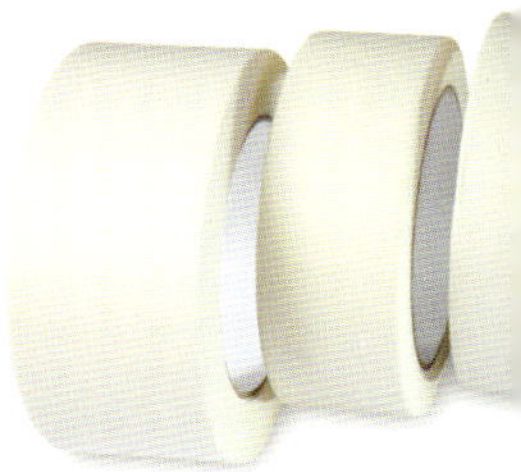

Use masking tape to block off any areas that you don't want painted. You can create crisp, clean paint lines by cutting a shape out of tape with a utility knife. Firmly press the tape onto the stone where you want the lines or shapes to be, then paint over them. When the paint is dry, peel off the tape. Voilà!

Erasing Mistakes

Painting a base color for your rock art is the best way to ensure mistakes can be easily "erased." If the mistake is still wet, wipe it away with water and a brush or cotton swab. If the paint is dry, try lightly sanding the mistake off with fine sandpaper or an old emery board, clear away any dust, and repaint the area with the base coat color to start again.

Preserving Your Art

I recommend you apply a final clear coat of protective finish over your rock painting. You can purchase these finishes at your local craft or hardware store, and they'll help protect your art from chipping, fading, and everyday wear and tear. This is especially useful if you plan to handle your stones, keep them outdoors, or leave them exposed to direct sunlight.

Protective finishing products differ, so do follow the directions for use on the package. Generally, however, you need to wait until all paint is dry, then apply an even coat of the clear finish as the final step in your rock-art creation. Affix any other decorative items (sparkles or sequins, for example) to the stone after the finish has been applied.

Ready, Set, Glow!

Now, let's dive into the beautiful rock-painting projects! As with all art, experimentation and lots ofpractice is key to creating brilliant, luminous works of art. Have fun!

Balance Cats

Create a happy balance with this adorable pair of intertwined kitties! This stone makes a perfect little gift for the cat lovers in your life—if you can bear to part with it, of course!

YOU WILL NEED

- Pencil
- Drawing compass
- Stone
- Paint: white, black, and glow paint
- Large and small paintbrushes
- Protective finish

1 Using a pencil and drawing compass, draw a circle on your stone. Fill in the circle with white paint, and allow this to dry, then draw another, slightly smaller circle 1–2 mm inside the first. Paint over the border of the smaller circle with a thin black line.

2 Now, pencil in the kitty design: draw the tail of one cat at the bottom of the circle, coming from the left, and the tail of the other cat at the top of the circle, coming from the right.

3 Once you're happy with the tails, draw in the rest of the cats as shown. The paw of the right cat forms the neck area of the left cat and vice versa. Draw little hearts for the ears and noses, add lines for the closed eyes, and don't forget the whiskers. Cute!

4 Next, use a small brush and black paint to fill in the cat on the right-hand side, and paint the tail at the bottom black too. Once the paint has dried, use a fine paintbrush and white paint to go over the cat's eye, ear, nose, and whiskers. Paint the white cat's features in black.

5 When the paint is dry, coat all the white areas (including the black cat's facial features) with a thin layer of glow paint. Allow this to dry, then repeat the process once or twice more. Finally, charge the glow paint on the stone and turn out the lights to check for any areas that need extra glow. Refresh the black features of the white cat and touch up anywhere else that may need it. When all the paint is dry, cover your kitty creation with a coat or two of protective finish.

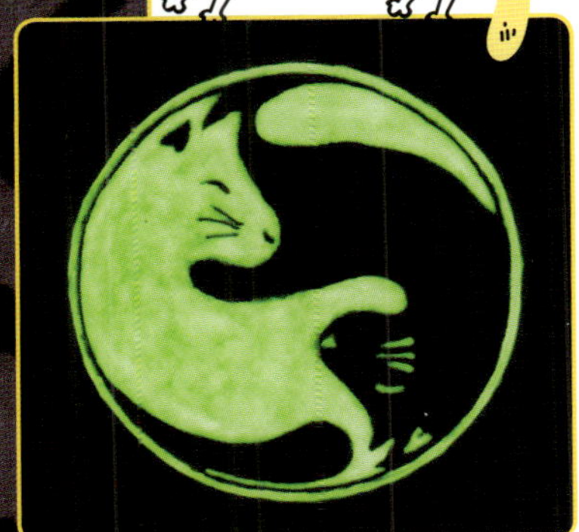

Triangle Twinkle

This rainbow geometric dot design is sure to catch your eye both night and day!

YOU WILL NEED

- Pencil
- Ruler
- Stone
- Paint: black, white, yellow, pink, purple, blue, orange, green, and glow paint
- Large and small paintbrushes
- Dotting tools in a range of sizes from small to large
- Protective finish

1 Using the ruler and pencil, draw a large equilateral triangle in the center of the stone. Fill the triangle with black paint for a base coat. When the paint dries, pencil in a small, upside-down triangle within the original triangle, placing its corners at the midpoint of each side.

2 Next, draw long lines from each corner of the large triangle inward, to meet in the center. Now, draw another small triangle pointing upward, its corners aligning with the long lines. The result will be a six-pointed star shape or hexagram; join the outside corners of this star to create a hexagon shape.

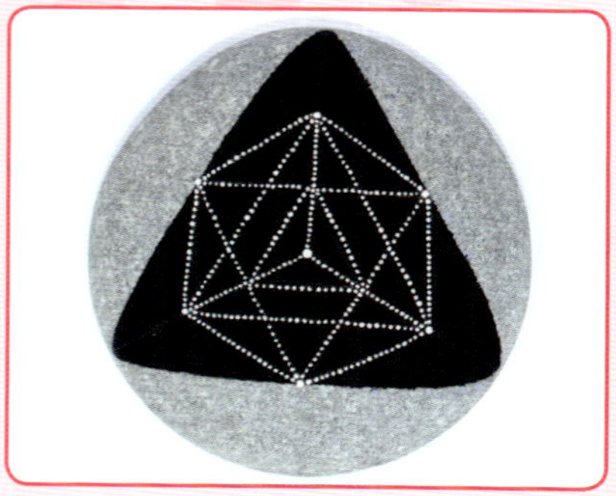

3 Now, pencil a smaller upside-down triangle in the middle of the six-pointed star, as shown. Start making dots using a small dotting tool and white paint. Start in the center, follow the lines to the corners of the star, then dot around the outside of the hexagon, and you have a cube! Finish adding dots along the lines in the hexagon.

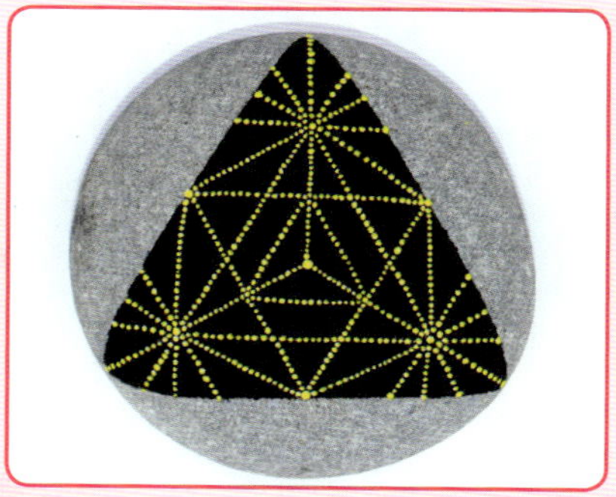

4 Dot the lines from the hexagon points to the corners of the large black triangle, then create new lines that radiate from the hexagon corners, continuing the lines within the hexagon. When all the white dots are dry, carefully dot over each one with yellow paint.

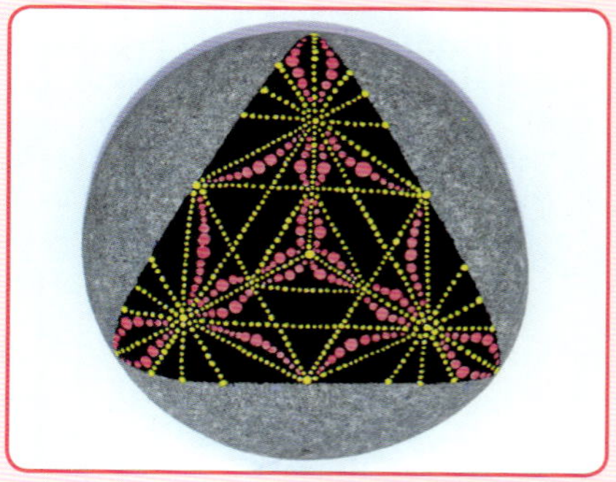

5 Add more dots in the design with white paint. From the center dot toward the corners, dot down the yellow line with curved lines of dots that start small, become larger in the middle, and then get smaller again. Make these dots in each section along the yellow line to the corners, and also make curved lines of dots along the inner sides of the hexagon. Paint these dots pink.

6 Continue making dots with white paint. Focus on one corner of the large black base triangle at a time, pointing the corner you are working on toward you. Fill each of the little sections between the pink and yellow dotted lines with dots of different sizes that taper to fit. You can do whatever you like, but copy what you have done on each side, so that the design is the same in all three corners. Once the white primer paint is dry, you can add the colors over the top. From the inside to the corner tip, the colors I've used in order are: purple, blue, orange, green, blue, white, purple. Paint the same in the remaining corners of the design.

7 Add more white dots around the small center triangle, then, from the edges of the center triangle to the outer edge of the main triangle, dot Y shapes. Add three more dots in the space left around the center icon. Once the white paint is dry, color the Y shapes orange, purple, blue, green, and yellow. Make the three dots in the center yellow as well.

8 When all your dot work is colored and dry, add glow paint. You can use a thin paintbrush to brush on a line of glow paint over the tiny yellow dots, and use a dotting tool to put glow paint on all the other colored dots. When the glow paint is dry, check to make sure you haven't forgotten any dots and do any other last touch-ups. Then, protect your colorful, tetrahedral rainbow-burst artwork with a coat or two of protective finish!

HANDY HINT

I recommend that you fix any misshaped or misaligned dots and make any other necessary adjustments as you go. That way, you don't have to make too many alterations at the end!

Dream Galaxy

Create this unicorn silhouette on a galaxy stone and, when the lights go out, you'll be holding a little piece of magic right in your hands!

YOU WILL NEED

- Stone
- Paint: black, white, neon pink, neon blue, neon yellow, and glow paint
- Paintbrush
- Pencil
- Masking tape
- Craft knife
- Small sponge
- Toothbrush
- Dotting tool
- Protective finish

1 Paint the entire top and sides of the stone with a black base coat. Allow this to dry, then add another coat of black paint.

2 In pencil, draw the outline of a unicorn in the center of the stone. Use masking tape to cover just the unicorn shape, cutting the tape carefully around the outline of the shape using a craft knife.

3 Using the sponge, dab a small amount of white paint across the stone and right over the masked-off unicorn outline, blending it so it's blurry.

4 Now, using the sponge, dab and blur neon pink paint over the top of the white. You don't need to wait for the paint to dry here.

5 Create depth in your galaxy by dabbing some black paint sparingly over the pink and white, to darken it along the sides. When the black paint dries, blur more neon pink over the top.

6 Continue to add colors to the galaxy with the sponge, using neon blue and neon yellow paint. Dab the blue paint to blend in with the pink for a purple haze, and blend yellow paint into the blue for a hint of green. There's no real map to the coloring: just try to keep the brightest area in the center, around the unicorn outline.

7 Use your glow paint to create stars! Dip the bristles of the toothbrush in glow paint, then hold the brush 2–3 in. (5–7 cm) from the stone and run your finger across the bristles toward you. This will flick tiny bits of glow paint (stars!) at the stone. Add some larger stars with a dotting tool, then repeat the star splatter using white paint, to create stars that are visible in the daylight.

8 Using a paintbrush, add a thin layer of glow paint along the edge of the unicorn outline, and check your work in the dark. Add more stars if necessary. When all paint is dry, peel away the masking tape to reveal the unicorn silhouette! Touch up the unicorn's inside edges using black paint and let this dry as well. Finally, protect your star-studded dream stone with one or two coats of protective finish!

HANDY HINT

When checking your glow work, snap a photo of your stone while it's glowing to use as a reference for your edits when the lights are back on.

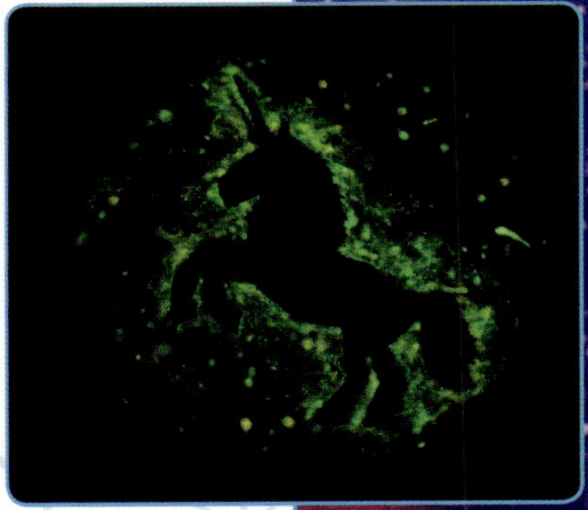

Luminosi Tree

Branch off from making dots and create this tree design. When night falls, so do the leaves, to reveal the "light-hearted" glowing design.

YOU WILL NEED

- Stone
- Paint: white, black, blue, green, yellow, orange, pink, and glow paint
- Pencil
- Paintbrush
- Protective finish

1 Start by drawing a large oval shape centered on the stone, and fill it with two coats of white paint for the base coat.

2 Use a pencil to draw in the tree trunk and branches. Draw the tree so that it forks at the center of the oval and the branches form a heart shape. Draw branches and roots that extend outside of the oval, and paint these branches with white base coat. Trace over the outlines of the tree with a thin line of black paint.

3 Paint the lower part of the background with blue paint. Paint some blue around the bottom branches and inside the heart as well. Dab dots of white paint around the top of the branches for the leaves. Go around the oval shape with a thick black outline.

4 Use white paint to prime the leaves of the tree. With a small brush or dotting tool, make small heart shapes around the ends of the branches. Position some of the leaves so that they overlap each other and cross the oval border onto the bare stone. Leave the tree trunk and branches visible.

5 Outline the individual heart-shaped leaves with a thin black outline. Begin adding colors in the leaves with a small paintbrush. Paint shades of darker green in the uppermost leaves, gradually changing to lighter shades of green as you move down.

6 Follow the light green with yellow, orange, and pink as you progress to the lower leaves. When the paint dries, add another coat to the leaves and touch up any white still showing through the very top of the tree with small dots of green and yellow.

7 Add different colors of fallen leaves around the bottom of the trunk outside the oval and outline them with a thin black line. Paint a faint light orange tint to the trunk and tree limbs. When this is dry, paint a coat of glow paint on the trunk and branches only. Allow to dry between coats. While the glow paint dries, paint small dots of glow throughout the leaves and in the blue areas; make a small full moon in the upper tree area. Paint it thick enough that it will show when glowing but remain invisible in daytime.

8 Refresh the black outline of the tree and the oval outline where still showing. Refresh the outlines around the leaves that are most at the forefront, and any additional leaves that were added. Charge the glow paint and admire your tree in the dark. Check for places that may require touch-ups of glow paint. When all paint is dry, protect your art with one or two coats of clear finish.

Isometric Glow

Op-tickle your senses by creating this simple yet mind-bending optical illusion art design. It's much easier to produce than it looks!

YOU WILL NEED

- Drawing compass
- Pencil
- Stone
- Ruler
- Paint: white, blue, yellow, and glow paint
- Large and small paintbrushes
- Protective finish

1 First, use a drawing compass to help you pencil in a large circle, centered on the stone. Then, begin to pencil the geometric design, starting by drawing six connected diamond shapes in the center of the circle. The diamonds should all have equal sides measuring about ½ in. (1 cm).

2 Next, use a ruler to draw a ¾-in. (2-cm) horizontal straight line going from the tip of the upper diamond to the right. Turn the stone and repeat this line from the next diamond tip, then do the same for the remaining diamond tips, turning the stone as you go. This will help you focus on one part at a time. Make sure you keep all the lines equal in length, evenly spaced, and aligned parallel with other lines on the same plane.

3 Continue the design by connecting another set of lines slanting downward, each measuring a little over ½ in. (1.5 cm) long, and running parallel to the lines beside them.

4 From these lines, draw horizontal lines out to the circle's edge. Fill in the remaining lines as shown, then use a small, thin brush to paint over the pencil lines with white paint.

5 Once the paint has dried, use your larger brush to add a thin layer of white paint over the entire circle. This is your base coat; you should still be able to see your white painted lines through it.

HANDY HINT

Why not play around with mixing paint to create different shades? You can mix small amounts of blue into yellow paint to make a bright green, for example, and make colors paler by adding white paint.

6 Now add the color! Using one color at a time, paint all the shapes in the design, mixing yellow and blue to make the green. Try to leave a space between the colors so that the thin white outlines remain. Allow the paint to dry, then add additional coats if needed. Once you're happy with the colors and the paint has dried completely, refresh all the white outlines, including the circle outline.

7 Last, add one or two coats of glow paint on all the white lines—charge the glow to check whether any lines are uneven, and touch them up if needed. Let the glow paint dry before you protect your luminous op-art with a coat or two of protective finish.

Glow Up

A layered, rainbow-colored mandala that shines from the inside, the white glowing background of this dotted design creates a very different, bright look!

YOU WILL NEED

- Stone
- Paint: white, light purple, bright blue, blue, bright green, yellow, orange, pink, purple, and glow paint
- Paintbrush
- Dotting tools in a range of sizes from small to large
- Protective finish

1 Start by painting a base coat over the visible area of the stone, using two coats of white paint. When this is dry, paint two or three layers of glow paint over the white, allowing time to dry between each one. Charge the paint and check to make sure you have a good, even glow before you go on to the next step.

HANDY HINT

With this design, when you fix mistakes, don't forget to make sure the glow coat underneath is still uniform with the rest. Add more glow paint if need be!

2 Use a large dotting tool to make the center dot in light purple paint, then surround this with tiny, evenly spaced dots in the same color.

3 Add the next ring of dots using bright blue paint. Position these dots between each dot of the first ring, lined up exactly below the spaces. Now, continue dotting the entire stone in this alternating dot pattern. As you span out with each new ring, gradually increase the size of the dots to cover the stone.

4 On my stone, the next two rings of dots are blue, then there are three rings of bright green, followed by one ring each of bright yellow, orange, pink, purple, blue, and back to green and bright yellow—repeating until the top and sides of the stone are covered. Add a large purple dot in the center of the stone.

5 When all the paint has dried, add a second coat if needed. Then, begin to add new dots over each colored dot in a slightly smaller size, using a lighter shade of the same color, made by mixing a little white paint into the color.

6 Add a darker dot of purple to the center dot, inside the lighter purple dot. To finish, add tiny dots of glow paint in the spaces between each of the colored dots to give you maximum effect when the lights go out! When all the paint is dry, protect your art with one or two coats of protective finish.

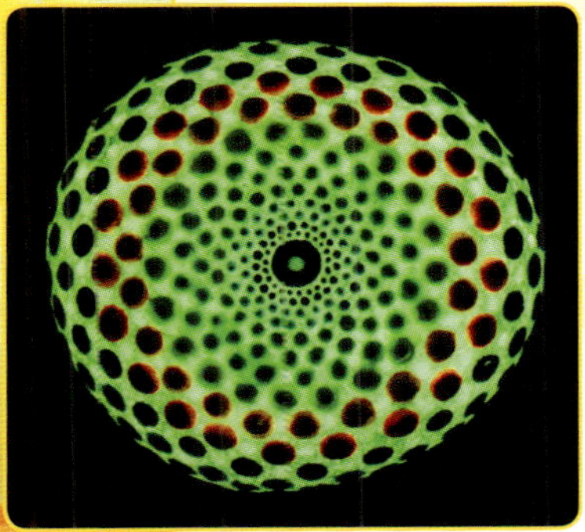

Fantastic Fungi

Did you know there are real-life mushrooms, snails and other living organisms that glow in the dark? It's called "bioluminescence"! In this project, you'll paint your very own bioluminescence-inspired marvelous mushroom scene!

YOU WILL NEED

- Stone
- Large and small paintbrushes
- Paint: white, black, neon blue, neon yellow, neon red, neon green, neon orange, and glow paint
- Pencil
- Small dotting tool
- Protective finish

1 Using your bigger paintbrush, paint a large white oval base coat over the center of your stone. Leave approximately ½–¾ in. (1–2 cm) of bare stone as a border. Allow to dry, then add another coat for good coverage.

2 Use a pencil to lightly draw in the mushroom scene. If any parts of your drawing go beyond the white oval onto the bare stone, use white paint to fill these areas.

HANDY HINT

Not confident in your drawing skills? Carbon transfer paper (available from craft and stationery stores) is your friend! Just print out a royalty-free picture you love, tape the printout to your stone with some transfer paper underneath, then trace the outlines with a pencil. Voilà—they're magically transferred to the stone!

3 Use a small, thin brush and black paint to trace over the main outline of your sketch, then outline the black dots on the mushroom caps as well. You can tidy up any mistakes or uneven lines by using white paint as an "eraser."

4 Now, paint in your colors! Begin by painting the background neon blue, then paint the tops of the mushrooms neon red and the underside of the caps neon yellow. Leave the bottom edge of the caps and the dots white. Paint any grass neon green.

5 Paint the snail's body neon orange with yellow dots throughout. Paint its shell neon yellow, then allow the stone to dry. Using your thin brush or a dotting tool, add glow paint to the white dots and white rims of the mushroom caps. Then, apply a single, thick coating of glow paint over the lower parts of the two mushroom stems at the front of the scene. While the glow paint is still wet, use the thin brush to paint horizontal stripes of white paint over the top, then immediately use a clean thin brush or a dotting tool to drag lines through the stripes from top to bottom. This will create a swirl pattern.

6 Repeat the technique in step 5 on the snail shell, to create swirls of glow and white paint. When the paint dries, the glow will appear yellow in daylight.

7 Paint lines of glow underneath the mushroom caps, and add some "rays" of glow to the blue background by painting vertical lines of glow paint on it. Add some glow paint to the snail's body, the grass blades and the remaining mushroom stems. Add some neon yellow to the fringed rings that sit at the top of each mushroom stem. Charge the glow under a light, then check in the darkness whether you need to make any adjustments or add more coats of paint. Once you're happy with it, retouch the black outlines and allow all paint to dry overnight before adding a coat or two of protective finish.

Mermaid Moment

Ah, the life of a mermaid: all bubbles and no troubles! Take a moment to make this daydream a reality by creating this glowing design on stone.

YOU WILL NEED

- Pencil
- Drawing compass
- Stone
- Paint: white, light blue, blue, yellow, black, bright pink, and glow paint
- Fine-tipped paintbrush
- Small paintbrush
- Protective finish

1 Use a drawing compass to pencil in a circle, off-center in the upper part of the stone. The circle needs to fit the mermaid, while leaving room for her tail outside the circle. Draw two or three smaller circles on the upper edge for the bubbles, then fill in the circles with white paint for a base coat. Paint a thin white line around the main circle.

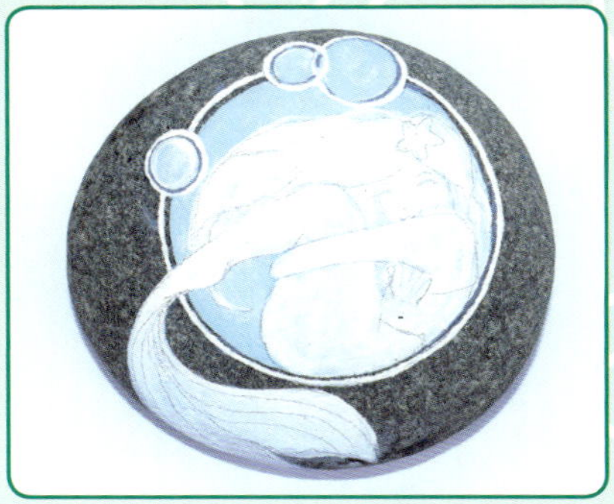

2 Add thin white borders around the bubbles. When the white paint is dry, use pencil to lightly draw the figure of a mermaid sitting inside the large circle, with her tail extending out into the stone. Paint the background and bubbles light blue and use white paint to prime the mermaid.

3 Paint the main colors of the mermaid, starting with the tail. Color the entire tail blue, with an emphasis along the edges. Allow this to dry, then paint yellow down the middle of the tail, blending it out to the edges to create a bright yellow-green shading.

4 Paint her hair yellow, then add streaks of white paint over the top. While you're at it, add a very light yellow tinge to the skin as well.

5 Using a fine-tipped paintbrush, add a thin outline in black paint between the different colors used on the mermaid, and mark in the facial features and other details. Use white paint to help contour the black outlines and even them up where necessary.

6 Use the small paintbrush to add bright pink streaks to the hair and around the tail fin. Apply small amounts at a time and blend with the other colors to create orange and purple. Add a bit of pink color to the cheeks, lips, shell bikini, and star hair ornament. Add orange dots to the star hair ornament.

7 Add the final small details: yellow dots on top of the orange in the star, and pink and yellow dots in the tail. Touch up the black outlines and add more streaks in her hair. Try to make sure everything looks the way you want it before you add the glow paint.

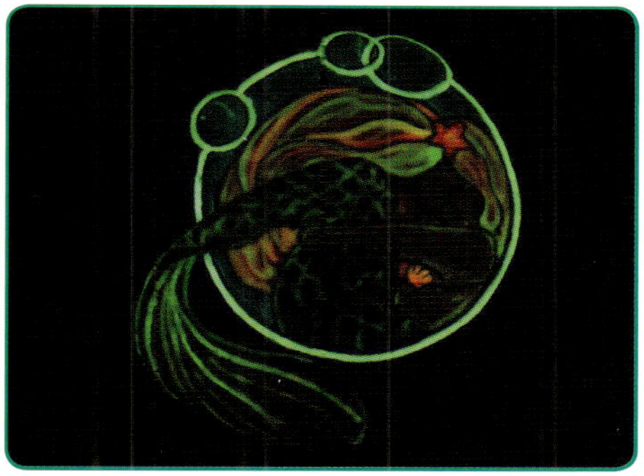

8 Now it's time to make your mermaid glow! Using a small paintbrush, add long lines of glow paint through the hair and tail fin, beginning in the center and working outward. Paint scales throughout the tail, and add thick lines of glow paint over the white outline of the circle border and bubbles. Highlight the star hair ornament and shell bikini with glow paint. Check the glow in darkness and make any adjustments needed.

9 When the paint is dry, cover your mer-mazing rock art with one or two coats of protective finish, and position your mermaid wherever you want a magical reminder of the sea—and its phosphorescence!

HANDY HINT

Be creative! Why not try adding metallic paint, sparkles, sequins, or tiny shells and other treasures found at the beach to decorate your mermaid and make her unique?

Congratulations!

Great job, glow-getter—you really know how to light up a room!

Now that you've completed these glow-in-the-dark rock projects, what will you do with your shiny new finished art pieces? The possibilities are endless!

May I suggest that the first thing you do is have a photo shoot? Take photos of your painted stones in the light and glowing in the dark, and share them on social media, to inspire others with your luminous creativity! And don't stop there: why not give them as gifts to friends and family, or leave them around your neighborhood to brighten a stranger's day?

Another amazing option is to place your stones in a row along the side of a path or hallway, to guide your way in the dark. If you set up a blacklight as well, they'll keep "glowing" even longer.

I hope you'll use what you've learned in this book to come up with your own unique rock designs, too. Whether you keep your art rocks for your own collection or send them off into the night, glow forth and create!

About the Author

Katie Cameron lives and creates in Halifax, Nova Scotia, on Canada's east coast. Katie is a self-taught rock artist—and glow and behold, this is her sixth painted rock tutorial book since 2015. She's positively beaming with excitement!

Keep shining, and don't forget to think happy dots!